Poems and Other Nonsense

Poems and Other Nonsense

Dexter Satterwhite

Rev. date: 04/09/2018

To order additional copies of this book, contact:
Xlibris
1-888-795-4274
www.Xlibris.com
Orders@Xlibris.com
775596

CONTENTS

When Mary Turned Forty

Time seems to fly,
The years sail on by,
Perhaps with mild depression.

Then "Father Time,"
Decides its time,
To teach us a valuable lesson.

We call it a milestone,
That we've lived this long,
And still be alive and kicking.

But the truth you see,
May just plain be,
Any moment the ticker could stop ticking.

As you stand at the edge,
Of this vast high ledge,
Which is commonly known as forty.

You must keep in perspective,
The whole big objective,
And remember that life's a big party.

Don't take it so seriously.
Don't fret on it so fiercely.
You've got to take this in stride.

Look at the bright side.
Think of the light side.
'Cause now, there's no place to hide.

Forty has come.
Don't look so glum.
Nobody's handing you a harp.

Look at it this way.
From now on it's a field-day.
In ten years, you can join AARP!

Dexter C. Satterwhite Jr.

January 1989

Dunes

Winds blow,
Sands flow,

    Like a mighty river meandering to the sea.
    These great mounds of silica,
    Crawl ever so slowly, slowly,
    Toward a destination only the wind can foresee.

Ever changing,
Rearranging,

    Like a young girl growing old.
    The wind does its work, day by day,
    As these almost living monoliths change by the hour,
        Into new monarchs not foretold.

Irresistible,
Irrepressible,

    Like an incoming tide.
    The sand moves at its own patient pace,
    Covering both living and dead,
    Guided by the wind it rides.

Immortal,
Eternal,

Like the wind and rain.
Though a man's time is fleeting,
Through the countless millennia,
The shifting sands remain.

Winds blow,
Sands flow.

Dexter C. Satterwhite Jr.

February 1989

Valentine Poem 1989

Rhyme and verse,
Of tragedy and mirth,
Have been written down through the years.

It warms the heart,
Makes life seem a lark,
And sometimes moves us to tears.

Poets old and new,
One thing they all knew,
Was mankind and his dealings.

And that syntax and meter,
There's simply no neater,
Way to express one's feelings.

So open this book,
And take a good look,
At this fine poetry.

And when you do,
I hope that you,
Will always remember me.

Dexter C. Satterwhite Jr.

February 1989

My Son

My son is a fair haired little boy,
With eyes as blue as the sky.
My son is a clever little boy,
And sometimes he's rather sly.

Sometimes when he wants his way,
He pits me against his mother.
And if that doesn't work, it's safe to say,
He'll try another ploy, and yet another.

My son is a learned little boy,
He makes good grades in school.
To his teachers, he's no bundle of joy,
'Cause he thinks he's pretty cool.

My son's a mischievious little boy,
And sometimes it gets him in trouble!
But then he's anything but coy,
And he'll makeup on the double.

My son's an easygoing little fellow,
He's liked by a lot of kids.
My wife thinks, at times, he's a little too mellow,
But I like him just the way he is.

My son's "the apple of my eye,"
"A chip off the old block" and such.
Though my patience, it's true, he can sometimes try,
I love him very much!

Dexter C. Satterwhite Jr.

April 1989

The Killer Bees

There's a terror coming from way down south.
I heard it on the radio and TV and by word of mouth.
It's coming as sure as the southern breeze.
It's those dastardly, devilish killer bees.

They've evil minds; they swarm like crazy.
When it comes to stinging, they're anything but lazy.
But when it comes to pollinating our flowers and crops,
That's when, it seems, their energy stops.

It all began down in Brazil,
On a research laboratory windowsill.
The scientists were careless; the bees were free,
And they started on their destructive spree.

That was thirty years ago.
Now they're in northern Mexico.
They've left a path of devastation.
Now their taking aim at our own nation.

They'll come in hoards and waves and swarms,
Destroying our homes, our towns, and our farms.
We can try to build a defensive line,
But they can't be stopped; it's the end of time.

They'll rape and pillage and murder and maim,
From California to the State of Maine.
And at the end to the mayhem and slaughter,
They'll enslave our sons and carry off our daughters.

And when their battle with man is through,
They'll be our masters, and the world they'll rule.
And who knows what they'll have in plan,
For what is left to the race of man?

But they won't get me without a fight.
I know I'm on the side of right!
They'll find my body after my last stand,
Still clutching a flyswatter and a Black Flag can!!

In the future, will anyone be left to tell,
Of this scourge that came from the gates of hell?
Worse than the old Bubonic Plague fleas,
Those menacing, diabolical killer bees.

Dexter C. Satterwhite Jr.

April 1989

Upon Visiting the Presbyterian Church

We committed a mortal sin last week!
We visited another church.
Now the rumors are out; there's simply no doubt.
We're leaving our brethren in the lurch.

No matter we've been members for seventeen years.
No matter that I'm on the board.
No matter that my wife teaches Sunday School,
And I give as much as I can afford.

No, something must be wrong with us.
How in the world did they fail?
Why have we turned our back on our faith,
And we're taking the road to hell?

If they only knew the truth of it all,
They would plainly see,
What our intentions really were,
And that we're as innocent as can be.

That our son is going to summer camp with a friend,
And we decided before we sent him,
Since the Camp Director was preaching that week,
It would be nice to go and meet him.

But now, the members think we're leaving the church,
And the Presbyterians think they've got us.
Everyone seems to have things figured out.
Everyone else but not us!

If they would take out their Bibles,
And read the words to the Teacher,
They'd see all the faithful make up his Church,
And I wouldn't be expecting a call from the preacher!

Its sad when wild talk gets things all confused,
And that's certainly not what we want.
So now we're in the middle of a fine mess.
We're damned if we do and damned if we don't.

Dexter C. Satterwhite Jr.

April 1989

Requiem for a Mustache

I lost a friend this morning,
That I have known so long!
No closer friend a man ever had,
One that never did me a wrong.

It greeted me every morning,
And at night when I washed my face.
It was quiet and polite and never complained,
And always knew its place.

It lived between my nose and lip,
And made me look somewhat older.
I kept it trimmed and brushed and fit,
And it kept my lip warm when the weather turned colder.

I had this friend for fourteen years.
It was so much a part of me,
That now it seems quite strange indeed,
It's not there for all to see.

This morning it died by my own hand.
A flick of the razor cut it free.
Some kill for hate or revenge or love,
But my reason was vanity.

You see, I thought at my age,
Living without it might make me look younger.
But instead, every line on my face stood out,
A fact that made me ponder.

As it lay there lifeless in the sink,
My heart was filled with regret.
I washed it into the septic tank,
But the memory I'll never forget.

In our darkest hour of sin and strife,
It's wise to seek guidance from Above.
I have no better excuse than this,
"We always hurt the one we love!"

Dexter C. Satterwhite Jr.

May 1989

My Yard
Or
Hell's One and One Half Acre

I go to work each morning,
For nine hours of the day.
I do this five days of the week,
So I can collect my pay.
That I might earn a living,
I toil and slave so hard.
Then exhausted, I drag myself home,
To begin working in my yard.

It stretches out before me.
Defiantly it sits and waits,
For all my feeble efforts,
With lawnmower, weed-eater, and rake.
I'm facing at least ten hours,
Of blood, sweat, and tears.
This yard is grinding me under,
And aging me beyond my years.

The grass has grown six inches,
In a little less than a week!
The weeds and thorns in the flower beds,
Must be ten inches deep!!
The storm we had the other day,
Blew at least a thousand limbs down!!!

They're laying everywhere out there,
Among the fire ant mounds!!!!

My first hurtle is the lawnmower:
Only three years old and already worn out.
If I could just get started without major repairs,
But that's something I very much doubt.
I really can't blame the maker,
For its condition so shabby and depraved.
It's been as reliable as I could have expected.
This yard drove it to its grave.

My yard is winning the battle.
I'm losing my sense of worth.
I've lost my love of life and fear of hell,
I've got it right here on earth.
When I bought this place, I didn't know,
I'd be keeping up Central Park!
If this is southern living,
I think I'll move to New York!!

Dexter C. Satterwhite Jr.

June 1989

Alphabet Poem

A
Bigamist
Carelessly
Decadent,
Engaged
Fair
Grace
Hill
In
June.

Knowing
Lady
Marie
Noble
Offered
Promise
Quite
Remarkably
Soon,

Though
Utterly
Vexed
Wed

Xavia
Yannah
Zaboon!

Dexter C. Satterwhite Jr.

July 1989

Alta Monte

High on a hillside,
Above the Middle Saint Vrain,
Stands a little cabin,
The place to which we came,

For rest and relaxation,
A break from city strife,
A chance to forget our troubles,
Maybe get a new "lease on life."

They call it Alta Monte.
I don't know what that means.
But now I can close my eyes,
And see it in my dreams.

Nestled there on the hillside,
Beneath the spruce and pine,
With the roar of the river down below,
We were lost between space and time.

The chipmunks rustled in the grass;
The hummingbirds came and went.
Mother Nature sang her "Siren Song,"
Which was exactly our intent.

The time went by and then ran out.
We had to go back home.
But we'll carry the memory of this place,
No matter where we roam.

As I sit here writing down this rhyme,
I hope I may impart,
The feelings from deep within my soul;
Alta Monte stole my heart.

Dexter C. Satterwhite Jr.

July 1989

Anniversary Poem 1989

Seventeen years of married life!
Seventeen years and only one wife!
Most unusual for this day and age,
Most marriages don't even get close to this stage.

It's a sad observation of modern life.
There's so much family trouble and marital strife.
With all the marriages that seem to go wrong,
Ours must be special for lasting so long.

So on this day when our feelings should show,
There is one thing I would like you to know.
Even if marrying you had been a sin,
I'd do the same thing all over again.

Dexter C. Satterwhite Jr.

July 1989

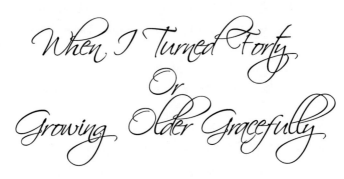

When I Turned Forty
Or
Growing Older Gracefully

O.K., I'm forty, so what!
When I think of the blessings I've got.
Being forty's not so bad,
With all the times that I've had,
You'd think, by now, I'd really be shot.

As for losing my looks, I don't care,
As I gaze in the mirror and stare.
When I take a good look,
At this nose like a hook,
There were no looks to loose, so there.

My golf game is not getting bad.
There's no reason for me to be sad.
It is really no worse;
It was always a curse.
I can't lose what I never had.

Some activities I have had to curtail,
Though my potency sure hasn't failed.
I'm still good for an hour,
Without a cold shower,
And finish up feeling just swell!

I am showing some signs of aging, I'm afraid.
I realize my life might be entering a new stage.
But that's neither here-nor-there,
For I still have my hair,
Which is more than I can say for some men my age.

My mind is still sharp I must say,
As sharp as it was in the old days.
Even though I've forgotten,
And off the subject I've gotten,
Uh, what was this poem about anyway?

Dexter C. Satterwhite Jr.

September 1989

Lament

Somewhere between sunset and twilight,
Between reality and fantasy,
Between the innocence of the Son,
And the love of the Father,
Mankind gropes in the eternal limbo,
Of knowledge squandered and perfection lost.

Blindly men stumble,
Down the twisting path of life,
In a headlong shamble,
Of greed, lust, envy, and hatred:
The path only ending at the Reapers feet.
His is the bitter harvest of life's autumn,
Whence comes death's cold and frost.

The world moves on through space,
Still cursed by war, famine, disease, and mistrust.
Will those of our species ever rise above this cesspool,
To end the centuries of misery and despair?
Or will man someday stop the world,
And cast himself off?

Dexter C. Satterwhite Jr.

October 1989

The Master's Question

Far from here in days gone by,
At Caesarea Philippi,
The one we call the Son of Man,
Wishing his Disciples to understand,
The role they'd play in God's great plan,
Asked them, "Whom do men say I am?"

They were quick to answer the Lord that day.
Each told what he'd heard other men say.
Some said "John the Baptist come back from death's bed."
Others said "Elijah or Jeremiah, or another profit long dead."
But wishing to look in their hearts instead,
"Whom do you say I am," He said?

And Peter never blinked an eye,
He faced his Savior in that day gone by,
And said, "You are whom the profits foretold,
So long ago in the days of old,
Who has come to the world to break Hades' hold,
To preach to men to save their souls."

And so the Disciples went far and wide,
To preach the Word of the One Who Died,
And Christianity grew and grew,
And before these men of God were through,
The whole known world knew what was true,
That Christ died on the Cross for me and you.

And so today we're to take a lesson,
From long ago and the Master's Question.
We're to spread His Word to all the lands,
To every tongue and race of man.
For He first put the Question to that tiny band,
"Whom do men say I am?"

Dexter C. Satterwhite Jr.

November 1989

The Perils of Thought

Upon this day I must confess,
I appear to be a man obsessed,
With this notion that I must possess,
A quiet place to take my rest,
And think about my life.

I don't seem to be happy anymore,
As I sit and stare at the bathroom door.
And my feet tap a little cadence on the floor.
And my posterior is starting to get sore.
This seat is cutting me like a knife.

But I have my deepest reflections on the throne.
Its one place I'm sure to be all alone.
There's no TV or radio or telephone:
Just me and my thoughts and a sore tailbone.
My legs are getting numb!

Well, philosophy's fine, but action's part of the plan.
I must get up while I still can,
And face the world if I'm able to stand.
I'm starting to feel like an entirely new man!
Its "onward and upward," and "up with the thumb!!"

Dexter C. Satterwhite Jr.

November 1989

Valentine Poem 1990

You are the passion of my heart,
The essence of my soul.
The reason for my every breath,
Is for you my heart to hold.

Our love has spanned some nineteen years;
We've felt life's joy, and sorrow, and shame.
Through all this happiness, and pain, and tears,
I hope you still feel the same.

I love you now as much as before.
If you should leave, my life would end.
Through all these years, my partner in life,
My wife, my lover, my friend.

Dexter C. Satterwhite Jr.

February 1990

The Cleansing Water

Oh, how I love to be,
Out of doors after a rain.
Water dripping from the leaves,
The dark color of the wet tree trunks that remains.

The sweet smell of the air,
Cleansed of the dust of the day.
I tell you, nothing can compare,
To the wet reflection of the sun's rays.

Just as the rain falls from Heaven,
To purify the work of God's Hand,
So does the Baptismal Pool,
Purify the soul of man.

The cleansing water takes our body.
The Good Lord purifies our soul.
Our sinful ledger is wiped clean.
We're free from Satan's deadly hold.

The Lord God planned it all this way,
Such a long, long time ago.
What more can one such as I say,
But thank you God for loving us so.

Dexter C. Satterwhite Jr.

March 1990

Time

I think I'll sit down and write a rhyme,
To explore the ins and outs of time.
I'll try to focus my whole attention,
On this mysterious thing called the "Fourth Dimension."

Has it always been here, or was there a beginning to time?
And if that is the case, will there be an end of some kind?
And what did we know of it before we invented the clock,
When man lived by his wits and a stick and a rock?
Later men rose with the sun and worked till it was gone,
'Till their lives were over, and they were nothing but bone.

Is time nothing more than an invention of man,
To help him formulate his plans?
Or are we at its beck and call?
Are we all slaves to the clock on the wall?
We're early for this; we're late for that.
We've scarcely the time to know where we're at.

Does the past exist only in our memory?
Is the future just how we expect things to be?
Does time only run in a constant line?
Or is it relative to the speed of light according to Einstein?
Does it bend with gravity as I am told?
Does it stand still in the midst of a Black Hole?
Will it continue until the stars from the heavens fall?
For that matter, does time really exist at all?

Though I may rave and scream and shout,
I'll never know what time is all about.
But one thing I do know, I must end this rhyme;
For alas you see, I've run out of time.

Dexter C. Satterwhite Jr.

March 1990

Mother's Day

So long ago you bore me.
I owe my very life to thee.

No matter what I do or say,
It's a debt I simply cannot repay.
But I make a poor gesture anyway,
And offer a gift on Mother's Day.

Dexter C. Satterwhite Jr.

May 1990

Mothers-In-Law

God created the world so long ago,
And then, He created man.
From man, He created woman.
It was all part of His Great Plan.

A man leaves his home for a woman,
And they lead a separate life.
Hand in hand, they grow old together,
Throughout life's toil and strife.

God knows that we're not perfect.
He can see our every flaw.
And so, that we might see them too,
He gave us a Mother-In-Law!

Dexter C. Satterwhite Jr.

May 1990

Teacher Retirement

Forty years of covering books.
Forty years of questioning looks.
Forty years of taking the roll.
Forty years of trying your soul.

Forty years of teaching a class.
Forty years of putting up with no sass.
Forty years of getting on their cases,
For forgotten homework and untied shoelaces.

Forty years of keeping them in line.
Forty years of a noisy lunchtime.
Forty years of preaching like Moses,
And treating those cuts, bruises, and runny noses.

Forty years of alphabetized seating.
Forty years of faculty meetings.
Forty years of papers to grade.
After forty years your debt's surely paid.

I'm not talking about Doctors, or Lawyers, or Preachers.
The profession I speak of is that of the Teacher.
And you've been one now for a mighty long time.
You've earned your retirement, and you'll like it just fine!

Dexter C. Satterwhite Jr.

May 1990

Comparing My Work to Shelley's

Mr. Shelley and I've both written a poem about time.
I sit and compare them, line for line.
I check them for meter, syntax, and rhyme.
I conclude that mine's better, every time.

As I sit in my smugness, I'm forced to take stock.
In the light of reality, I'm in for a shock.
With all of this talent I've supposedly got,
Why is his poem in this book, and mine is not?

Dexter C. Satterwhite Jr.

July 1990

On Flag Burning

Long you have waved, "o're the land of the free."
Why are there those who would destroy thee?
Who would rip you down from your lofty place,
To soil your stripes and your stars, deface.

You're the symbol of the nation that guarantees our rights.
We can say what we please and not fear for our lives.
When government actions make us cross,
Why take it out on a piece of cloth?
What good does it do to burn the flag:
To treat you as though you were only a rag?

As Christ had to die for the sins of creation,
Perhaps you're defiled for the sins of the nation.
But I see no reason for burning "Old Glory."
I've said my piece: end of the story.

Dexter C. Satterwhite Jr.

July 1990

History

History is something that's out of date.
That's what my son said about it.
It's something most folks don't appreciate,
But what would we all do without it?

Without our knowledge of Rome and Greece,
And the laws and learning they gave us,
It would set us back a thousand years at least,
With no modern conveniences to save us.

Without our understanding of the "Founding Fathers,"
And the creation of their vision and reason,
Why should we even bother,
With their esoteric concept of freedom?

For those who love history, it's a "Sacred Cow,"
But there are still those who just can't relate.
They live out their lives in the "here and now,"
And history is just something that's out of date.

Dexter C. Satterwhite Jr.

August 1990

When in the Course of Human Events

"When in the course of human events,"
We all, at long last, show some common sense,
And set aside our pride and our vanity,
To put an end to war's insanity,
Then all of this misery, we might circumvent,
"When in the course of human events."

"When in the course of human events,"
While putting food on the table and paying the rent,
We happen to notice our wives and children there,
And happen to show them how much we care,
We might build a stronger family covenant,
"When in the course of human events."

"When in the course of human events,"
While putting food on the table and paying the rent,
We happen to take notice of our fellow man,
And fight hunger and injustice whenever we can,
We might find our time to be very well spent,
"When in the course of human events."

"When in the course of human events,"
We choose to do nothing and sit here content,
To let mankind slip into the dismal abyss,
While we idly stand by in a self-induced bliss,
Then Satan will seem to be quite competent,
"When in the course of human events."

"When in the course of human events,"
When we've lived out our lives and we're haggard and bent,
Then death's cold touch lays us 'neath the sod,
And we stand that day before our God,
To explain the manner in which our lives were spent,
"When in the course of human events."

Dexter C. Satterwhite Jr.

August 1990

Mountain Biking in East Texas

I got myself a mountain bike.
I ride it day and night.
I don't know why I do it?
There's not a mountain in sight.

Dexter C. Satterwhite Jr.

September 1990

My Dog

I have a little black dog.
Scottish Terrier is his breed.
His kind comes from the "misty isle:"
An old, old pedigree.

They were bred to root out badgers,
With snout, and tooth, and claw.
Trouble is we've got no badgers,
Our region's only flaw.

So he takes it out on cats and toads,
And whatever is in his path.
If any thing happens to get in his way,
It's sure to feel his wrath.

That is if he is certain,
It's a weaker thing than he.
If not, he'll simply tuck his tail,
Turn on his heels and flee.

They say that dogs are loyal;
They'll stick to you like glue.
It's true he's always underfoot,
Like gum stuck to a shoe.

When I go to get a cookie,
He's right there at my feet.
Sitting there with those big brown eyes,
Looking as sweet as he can be.

I know he wants that cookie.
He can't put one on me.
I tell you that half a cookie,
Was as good as good could be.

I love my little black dog.
I've but to whistle and he comes running.
And I know he'll always love me back,
As long as the cookies keep coming.

Dexter C. Satterwhtie Jr.

September 1990

The Price of Freedom

When brother turned against brother,
And battlefield streams turned red.
When southern fields were covered,
With the bodies of the dead.
When the peace of the nation was smothered,
By sorrow and hatred instead.
And struck down by another,
"Honest Abe," shot through the head.

Our country was torn asunder,
Through the four years of the night.
And the guns did roar and thunder,
In a crescendo above the fight.
And the northern armies did plunder,
And trample the southern white.
And the nation that rose from under,
The ashes was unified.

Since the time of those desperate days,
The years number six score and five.
And the men on both sides did pay,
With their blood, and pain and lives.
And the lesson for us today,

Should come as no surprise.
If any man be kept a slave,
Then freedom cannot survive.

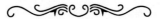

Dexter C. Satterwhite Jr.

October 1990

The Scots are Such a Cunning Race

The Scots are such a cunning race,
More clever than most men.
They've bred a breed of little dogs,
That look just like them.

Dexter C. Satterwhite Jr.

October 1990

Leaves

I'm up to my knees in leaves.
When I walk through them they make me sneeze.
They force me to shout,
And run all about.
God help me won't you please.

I've not seen the ground in weeks,
And they've not even reached their peak.
If any more leaves come down,
I think I will drown,
If first, I don't simply freak!

They're too deep for a mowing session,
And raking is out of the question.
If I tried it, I fear,
I'd be at it all year.
No, I need some new secret weapon.

And burning would do no good,
Even if I thought it would.
If I tried I, you see,
I'd end up in TDC,
Because I'd burn the neighborhood!

If you were me, and I were you,
Please tell me what you would do.

How would you relieve,
My drowning in leaves?
Oh tell me, please tell me true.

Dexter C. Satterwhite Jr.

November 1990

The Pot and the Kettle

Why for some is life so hollow,
That the bar trail they will follow?
And gin and whisky they will swallow,
'Till in the gutter they will wallow.

Eventually they end up in jail,
If no one will raise their bail.
All their lives their souls they sell,
'Till their life's a "living hell."

But, why do I think I'm so right,
When evil I refuse to fight?
I think I'm living in the light,
When my life's just as much a blight.

The truth is something we don't speak,
When more convenient a lie to seek.
Are not the strong to inherit the weak,
And never "turn the other cheek?"

Those who hate their fellow men,
For the color of their skin.
Do they think it not a sin?
Do we bear it with a grin?

Oh, it's easy to point the finger,
At all the souls run through life's ringer,
And all those stung by hardship's stinger,
And those whose pain and sorrows linger.

When people need our help today,
Do we turn and walk away?
Maybe we'll help another day.
It's not our problem anyway.

The devil also gets his due,
From "good folks" like me and you.
You don't think that this is true?
Just keep living the way you do.

Dexter C. Satterwhite Jr.

December 1990

Winter Wind

When "Winter" blows his icy breath,
We're at his mercy, more of less.
And prudent people should decide,
The proper course: to stay inside.

Yet, we wrap ourselves like polar bears,
And venture out into his lair,
And bend and strain with every gust,
And curse, in vain, his frigid lust,
And pull our hats low on our heads,
And watch the world turn brown and dead.

Dexter C. Satterwhite Jr.

December 1990

Words

You've always had a way with words,
With all of those less competent.
With your excellent choice of nouns and verbs,
There's no misunderstanding what you meant.

Your words pour forth like a driving rain,
Upon my ear and beaten brow,
Until I just might go insane,
Or threaten to up and leave you now.

You're like a summer thunderstorm,
But you're my woman, and I'm your fella'.
This doesn't look like a false alarm,
So where did I leave my umbrella?

Dexter C. Satterwhite Jr.

December 1990

Ski Trip

Wind and rain and ice and snow,
And down the road like fools we go.
Testing the limits of our very being,
And all so that we might go skiing.

Dexter C. Satterwhite Jr.

January 1991

Skiing

Hurtling down the slope on two thin sleds.
Your life is hanging by a thread.
And all the remnants of sanity have fled,
With only the bottom to reach.
Well I've done it, yes-sir-ee,
Big-as-life, for-all-to-see.
Proved I could, and believe-you-me,
Next time, I'll go to the beach!

Dexter C. Satterwhite Jr.

January 1991

Jock's Prayer

"Ma" Daddy's "goon'a" leave me,
And "ma Moomy" will "nay" stay.
"Ma Broother" will be off "tae" school,
Very soon today.
I am a sad "wee" Scotsman,
When "ma foolks" have "goon" away.
May the Good Lord bless and keep me,
Through this "loonly" day.

What's a "wee" man "tae" do,
When it's quiet as a "moos?"
It "jest sae" damn "depressin'."
It makes me want "tae shoot."
There's "nay" a "livin" thing,
Anywhere "aboot."
May the Good Lord bless and keep me,
In this "loonly hoos."

Sometimes I "git sae freightened."
What if "ma hoosy" burns!
This place is "cawld" and empty.
Have "ye nay" concern?
These days are "loong" and "loonly."

Where can a "wee" Scot turn?
May the Good Lord bless and keep me,
Till "ma foolks" return.

Dexter C. Satterwhite Jr.

February 1991

Love

A mother provides for her children.
She satisfies their every need.
At each cry, and sigh and whimper,
She'll be there to hear and take heed.
"But when you get right down to it;"
"When it comes to push and shove."
Of all the things a mother can give,
The most precious gift is love.

A man and a woman marry.
They make a promise to God.
They promise to live their lives together,
'Till they're laid beneath the sod.
Together, they face life's toil and pain,
With guidance from above.
One word can describe a bond like this,
And it is simply love.

Of all the "golden virtues,"
That people can possess,
There's one that most of us seem to lack,
I'm sorry to confess.
All we must do is open our hearts,

And God's grace will "descend like a dove."
Yes, "faith, hope, love abide, these three,
But the greatest of these is love."

Dexter C. Satterwhite Jr.

February 1991

Money

Upon a cross He hung,
Because His friend had lied.
Beneath the broiling sun,
He hung there till He died.

His friend betrayed their trust,
When money cast its spell.
And now it beckons us,
On toward the gates of hell.

For money cannot buy,
The things we really need.
Too often, it only provides,
Jealously, envy, and greed.

Love cannot be bought,
Nor loyalty guaranteed.
When money is all that's sought,
Destruction has planted its seed.

He ascended to His throne:
The Holy Son of Light.
And His friend now left alone,
Committed suicide.

Dexter C. Satterwhite Jr.

February 1991

Poetic Justice

Poetry is my hobby.
I write it all the time.
I love to explore the ins and outs,
Of syntax, meter, and rhyme.

I sure do love my hobby.
I turn out lots of verse.
But I fear, when it comes to quality,
It ranges from bad to worse.

Dexter C. Satterwhite Jr.

March 1991

Prayer

In evening time at the end of the day,
When the blue of the sky is fading away,
I stand and gaze at the setting sun,
When all my daily tasks are done,
And my mind will turn to thoughts of where,
I'll go to meet my God in prayer.

It needs to be a quiet place,
Where with clear mind and tranquil face,
I place my very heart and soul,
Completely within my Savior's control,
And I tell Him of my every care,
When I go to meet my God in prayer.

And when I'm through, the world I see,
Looks ever so much better to me.
And I'm ready to face another day,
Without regret nor further delay.
For I'm able to shed the burdens I bear,
When I go to meet my God in prayer.

So when sorrow grips you through and through,
Remember you can do the same thing too.
Just ask God's blessing for your fellow men,

And His forgiveness of your sin.
And you will find salvation there,
When you go to meet our God in prayer.

Dexter C. Satterwhite Jr.

March 1991

The Noblest of Birds

Soaring high across the sky,
Higher than I'd dare if I could fly.
Looking down upon the land,
At the low domain of man.
Far more noble than other fowl,
Than small bobwhite or hooting owl.
What a thrill but to possess,
A single feather from your nest.
You circle where the angles trod,
Just beneath the face of God.
Away from all terrestrial bound,
Creatures dwelling on the ground,
Who plod through dust, and mud, and snow:
The beaver, fox, and buffalo.

Can we reach as high as thee,
We of low humanity?
By working to help our fellow men,
Can we build the world again?
Can we make a better place,
Where all God's children will be safe?
To Bedan-Powell we give our thanks,
That you are Scouting's highest rank.
And to our forefather's revelation,
You are the symbol of our nation.
Dare we set our sights so high?

Dare we look right to the sky?
Oh bird of myth and majesty,
Do we dare to be like thee?

Dexter C. Satterwhite Jr.

March 1991

Awakened by a Storm

Black to white, it splits the night:
The jagged shape, the searing light.
It fills the very soul with fright,
At "Mother Nature" and her might.

For an instant, night is day:
The shroud of darkness torn away.
The weak of heart are left to pray,
Their inner fears to keep at bay.

Then "Thor's Hammer" sounds its knell,
Like the burst of a cannon shell,
Like the tolling of some giant bell,
Or the closing of the gates of hell.

No need to guess from whence it came,
With windows rattling in their frames,
And the only sound now that remains,
Is the howling wind and pouring rain.

Thrust from out of my slumber deep,
The shock is enough to make one weep.
Off to the window for a peek,
Then back to bed and back to sleep.

Dexter C. Satterwhite Jr.

May 1991

Our Little Sentry

Just like that, after a cat,
Especially if it hissed or spat.
Our little sentry guards our yard,
From all intrusion, be it this or that.

Always alert and never off duty,
Nothing gets by this vigilant cutie.
No vermin may enter his sacred domain,
And a biscuit or chew-stick serves as his booty.

For Heaven's sake, he's after a snake.
It's off to the garage for a hoe or a rake.
Life to the victor, death to the vanquished:
The spoils of war for a Scotty to take.

He works so hard at securing our yard,
And a pat on the head is his favorite reward.
The "Highland Soldier," Britain's elite:
No need to worry when he is on guard.

Dexter C. Satterwhite Jr.

May 1991

Anniversary Poem 1991

Nineteen years of marital bliss,
What more could one ask from life than this?
If I might be granted just one small wish,
From you, t'would be nothing more than a kiss.

Thank you for being my wife, my dear,
And sharing my dreams, and joy's, and tears.
And thank you for comforting and calming my fears,
And loving me in spite of myself all these years.

❧

Dexter C. Satterwhite

July 1991

Quiet at the Hyatt

Oh, it's quiet at the Hyatt.
There is nothing heard at all.
You could sleep right through a riot,
Though they're tearing down the walls!

Yes, it's quiet at the Hyatt.
You should really go and try it,
After all.

❧

Dexter C. Satterwhite Jr.

July 1991

Rejoice

Rejoice, the night is gone!
Rejoice, the sun has risen!
Upon this morn',
A child is born.
Our sins shall be forgiven.

A new day has begun,
With the songs of angels heard.
For by His birth,
'Tis God on earth,
To teach His Holy Word.

For man all by himself,
Has but the grave and bone.
Without his God,
Has but the sod,
When life on earth is gone.

An end to sin and death.
'Tis for us to make the choice.
Eternal Life,
In Paradise,
Rejoice my friends, rejoice!

Dexter C. Satterwhite Jr.

July 1991

Boston

Consider, if you will, the city of Boston.
You'd think, when pronounced, it should rhyme with Austin.
But not, as it seems, to the learned locals,
They'll quickly inform all us ignorant yokels.
"Baaston's" the name that was given their home,
By the Puritans who sailed across the foam.

And I guess they believe the letter R to be rotten.
For when it follows a vowel, it is simply forgotten.
Then cart becomes "caat," and card becomes "caad,"
And on Saturday morning, they all mow their "yaads."
And "Baaston" women sit and drink tea in their "paalas,"
And watch the ships sail in and out of the "haaba."

The traffic is just awful for all of the "caas."
And at night you can look up and see the "staas."
Or take in a ballgame at Fenway "Paak."
And after it's over, walk home in the "daak."
Or go to an Irish pub, and learn to throw "daats."
Or send your kid to "Haavad," if he or she is real "smaat."
Or just keep on living till you're an old "faat."
There's no doubt it; it's a city "apaat."

Some say that it's Heaven, but I'm not so bold.
But when the good die, they go to "Baaston," or so I'm told.

Dexter C. Satterwhite Jr.

August 1991

Break for Moose

"Break for Moose! It Could Save Your Life!"
That's what the signs say in Maine.
For they're lurking behind every rock and tree,
To bring you but sorrow and pain.
Are they angry that we are out in the wild?
Though I give it much thought, still it does beguile.
Can man and moose ever be reconciled?
If not, well then who is to blame?

Break for moose if you value your life,
Or you will surely come to grief.
You'll leave fatherless children and a widowed wife,
Probably on government relief.
It's all too clear that they just can't wait,
For the slightest opportunity to seal our fate.
Wake up; wake up before it is too late!
This is but my humble belief.

Dexter C. Satterwhite Jr.

August 1991

An Unexpected Lily

While working in my yard one day,
And wishing instead I was at play,
I was taken aback by what I did see,
For a lily stood where it should not be.

I rose and stared at that plot of land,
For it was not planted by my hand.
Eight years I've lived here on this place,
And never has it shown its face.

Yet standing there beside the fence,
With crimson bloom and petals dense,
Standing straight and standing proud,
As if to call to me out loud,
"Look at me, I have finally come,
Above the ground to see the sun."

How long was it there; how long did it wait,
For the chance to germinate?
Who planted it in days of yore?
There are some things worth waiting for.

Dexter C. Satterwhite Jr.

September 1991

The Rose

I went to where the flowers grow,
Put forth my hand and plucked a rose,
And took it to my dwelling place,
And placed it in a crystal vase,
And set it on my mantel high,
To be seen by every passer-by.

Its beauty shown like the morning dew,
But only for a day or two.
And though I wished for it to stay,
Alas it started to decay.
And its petals dropped one by one,
And it shriveled like dry grass in the sun.

And though I wish it were not so,
Time passes by as the four winds blow.
And the world continues to rearrange,
In a state of constant change.
And for all my begging and pleading,
Beauty, like fame, is fleeting.

Dexter C. Satterwhite Jr.

September 1991

Another Sonnet

I said future sonnets were out.
But this is the classical kind.
It just might challenge my mind,
And be something I could tout.
If I write a good one, I'll shout!
But only if it has some good lines,
In the proper meter and rhyme,
That's what poetry is all about.
But it can be somewhat tricky,
When writing in a new form.
I might find it somewhat constrictive.
Just fourteen lines: this is getting sticky.
I'm starting to find cause for alarm.
Boy, this form is restrictive!

Dexter C. Satterwhite Jr.

October 1991

In a Cemetery

They lie beneath these cold grey stones,
In this place of the dead.
These boxes filled with molting bones.
The soil and rock now form their bed.

They lived and worked on land and sea,
In joy and hope and pain and strife.
And here the saved lie fast asleep,
Free from the sorrow they knew in life.

The grass now grows above their heads.
Wild flowers bloom above their feet.
And theirs is the peace of God instead,
Though we alive bow our heads and weep.

Their souls will go to dwell on high.
The bodies that they now have shed,
Lie beneath my feet, and when I die,
I'll be brought here to join these dead.

Dexter C. Satterwhite Jr.

October 1991

Self Delusion

Black is white.
Day is night.
When you believe what you want to,
Everything's all right.

Dexter C. Satterwhite Jr.

October 1991

Skidders

Bring on the skidders;
Mow them down.
Knock the trees right to the ground.
Smash them, grind them, tear them up.
Their needed, you see, for lumber and pulp.

Take all the pines;
Haul them away.
Wreck all else that's in the way.
Take all of value the forest has got,
And leave the rest piled up to rot.

Dexter C. Satterwhite Jr.

October 1991

The Shakespearean Sonnet

Consider the Shakespearean sonnet,
The oddest form of verse.
To grace the word poetry upon it,
Is something that's simply perverse.
It can only consist of fourteen lines,
With every other in each stanza rhyming,
Except for the last two that also rhyme,
Which completely throws off my timing!
For one who thinks that a poem should flow,
Like a river meandering its curves,
The ending comes as quite a blow,
That certainly frays my nerves.
I swear by my honor and the Texas Blue Bonnet,
I shall never, ever write a Shakespearean sonnet.

Dexter C. Satterwhite Jr.

October 1991

Concrete

I'm just a slab of concrete,
Lying here beneath your feet.
And I'll be lying around,
Here on the ground,
When you're beneath me by six feet.

Dexter C. Satterwhite Jr.

November 1991

Standing in Awe

The Poet of all the Heavens,
Who writes the verse of time.
Creator of all things that we know,
The Father of mankind.

You flung the stars across the sky,
To form the Milky Way.
And sent the moon to rule the night,
The sun to rule the day.

You set the planets upon their paths,
Around their mother stars.
And guide the stars along their way,
No matter how near of far.

In all the reaches of this vast domain,
The stars of Your Creation shine.
And I stand in awe of how great you are,
And how very small am I.

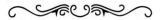

Dexter C. Satterwhite Jr.

November 1991

Nightfall

The sun sinks low in the west,
Toward an inevitable collision with the horizon,
Until it kisses the curving edge of the earth,
And sinks like a doomed ship in a dark sea.

And with it the day slowly dies,
But not like an invalid in a nursing home,
Or the dying embers of a neglected fire,
But in wild fury like an old moose,
Surrounded by hungry wolves.
First yellow then orange then red,
The sky explodes in crimson agony,
Like this fallen giant,
Dying by tooth and claw.

And just as the fallen beast eventually succumbs,
So does the light.
It slowly fades from the western sky,
As the creeping edge of darkness wins the battle.
And one by one the fair lights of night appear,
The stars, and then the "Mother of Night" herself,
The moon rises to claim her domain.
And long silken shadows creep across the land.

Dexter C. Satterwhite Jr.

December 1991

November Moon

Sparkling, glittering down through the trees,
Showering me with silver light.
Shimmering like an evening breeze,
On a cold November night.

Its face shines down upon the land,
Its glow caresses leaf and grass.
And there is ample light on hand,
To see obstructions that I pass.

The shadows dance across my lawn,
The blue-white disk above my head.
The ruler of the sky 'till dawn,
And here on earth am I instead.

I trace its path along its flight,
It fills my very soul with awe.
I wish I could stay out all night,
And watch it till the morning thaw.

Just once a month it shines so bright.
In days to come I will remember,
How it looks on this splendid night,
The frosty moon of late November.

Dexter C. Satterwhite Jr.

December 1991

Priorities

As I stand and gaze at the sunrise,
I know somewhere else the sun sets.
Where some are content and happy with life,
Others are filled with regrets.
When I see the joy of a young mother,
And hear her newborn baby cry.
I know somewhere else there's another,
Who watches her baby die.

I see a happy wedding,
And think ahead to innocence gone.
To a couple who's anger needs shedding,
Before they are both alone.
And I think of the millions of people,
Whose souls are lost in the night.
Who live their lives beneath the church steeple,
And never quite see the light.

I guess it's a matter of conviction.
God's work is ours to be done.
We can blame but ourselves for restriction,
In spreading the Word of His Son.
The task is ours for the taking.

We can build a new world by and by.
If not, as His children we're faking.
It's all up to you and I.

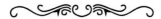

Dexter C. Satterwhite Jr.

December 1991

The Man on the Bench

He sat unmoving on the bench,
While passers-by gave berth to his foul stench.
And he stared at humanity's ebb and flow,
For he simply had nowhere else to go.

He sat all morning 'till half past one,
In the sultry air and broiling sun.
Then the air grew heavy, and the clouds hung low,
But he simply had nowhere else to go.

The lightening flashed, and the thunder came,
And the afternoon threatened a drenching rain.
And the rain poured down, and the wind did blow,
But he simply had nowhere else to go.

When the clouds finally parted, and the sun came out,
The people began to move about.
But the man sat slumped with his head hung low,
For he simply had nowhere else to go.

He was there all night and most of the next day,
With a body slowly wasting away.
And he died right there upon "Skid Row,"
For he simply had nowhere else to go.

Dexter C. Satterwhite Jr.

February 1992

Valentine Poem 1992

In this world of toil and sin,
What goes around comes back again.
And the things we cannot escape,
Are death, and taxes, and our fate.

Nineteen years is a long, long time,
For you to be my valentine.
So let me tell you what's in store,
You'll have to put up with me for nineteen more!

Dexter C. Satterwhite Jr.

February 1992

Writer's Block

I can't think of anything to write!
I've never been in such a plight.
Am I, or am I not a sight?
Yes, writer's block is such a fright,
When all one's thoughts have taken flight.

I'm just no better off than dead,
When nothing pops into my head.
My brain feels like a lump of lead.
I think I'll just put it to bed,
And explore the "Land of Nod" instead.

Dexter C. Satterwhite Jr.

February 1992

A Pressing Issue

Your pressing is distressing,
And I find myself confessing,
That it's all just quite depressing,
And furthermore, it's stressing,
Out my mind.

If you'd pay more attention to detail,
On these clothes I bought at retail,
I am sure it would compel,
You to consider your work well,
And take your time.

For your work is now so fleet,
You forget about the pleats,
And I cannot walk the streets,
With my ironing incomplete.
If my clothes were looking neat,
Then life would be so sweet,
And I'd be fine.

Dexter C. Satterwhite Jr.

March 1992

Good Advice

Drink and smoke,
And you will croak.
But as not to offend,
I didn't say when!

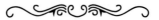

Dexter C. Satterwhite Jr.

March 1992

Leftover for Tomorrow

What will the future bring?
Will the maidens weep or sing?
Will those convinced they're right,
Still choose up sides to fight,
And let the "death bell" ring?

Just as in the days of yore,
When the world was torn by war,
Will the young men go to die,
And leave their loved ones to cry?
Is that what we have in store?

What wisdom can we borrow,
To end this shame and sorrow?
Or will our present hate,
Finally seal our fate,
And be leftover for tomorrow?

Dexter C. Satterwhite Jr.

March 1992

Lemmings

So lemmings don't really commit suicide.
They've never thrown themselves over the brink.
Instead, they practice infanticide.
It's a wonder they don't go extinct.
That's how they control their population;
They kill each other's young.
In order to limit their procreation,
They murder their neighbor's daughters and sons.
If they'd just take charge of their urges,
And practice some self-control,
They wouldn't have these murdering scourges,
And their young would have a chance to get old.
Looking back at my primal beginning,
I'm glad I'm not a lemming.

Dexter C. Satterwhite Jr.

March 1992

A Bowtie Guy

I want to tell you of my friend,
Even though he's not my kin.
He knows himself and knows his place:
A credit to the human race.
But more than this, he knows what looks good,
What compliments him as good clothing should.
His style is straightforward and never shy,
Because, you see, he's a bowtie guy.

He stands a head above the rest,
When it comes down to his dress.
For it speaks of a lower intellect,
To ware a noose around your neck.
It gets in your way when you stoop,
And tends to dribble in your soup,
And is soiled and stained with every sneeze,
And flaps over your shoulder in the breeze.

I must admit, I'm the closet kind,
For I do not wear one all the time.
But when the mood is right and my spirits fly,
I free myself for a normal tie,
And reach for the high place of my friend,

Even though he's not my kin.
He's looking sharp and feeling spry.
And best of all, he's a bowtie guy.

Dexter C. Satterwhite Jr.

April 1992

Climbing the Winding Stair

Life is like a stairway,
From birth right to the end.
There are only two ways that you can go;
You can climb it or you can descend.

To climb it takes some effort.
At times each step can seem great.
To descend is always easier,
But the last step ends at hell's gate.

So keep your eyes ever upward,
Pressing on with vigor and care.
Remember our Lord waits at the top step,
As you're climbing the winding stair.

Dexter C. Satterwhite Jr.

May 1992

The Saint Vrain

Time went by so fast,
Alas.
We scarcely realized,
It had past.

Held in the arms,
Of the valley's charms,
Through morning sun,
And afternoon storm.

Chipmunks pranced,
And sunbeams danced.
And we were held,
In nature's trance.

Our sanity regained,
If we could but remain,
On the middle fork,
Of the river Saint Vrain.

Dexter C. Satterwhite Jr.

June 1992

Along About August

I'm ready for fall,
Leaves and all.
The thermometer's soaring.
I'm heeding the call,
For gentle north breezes,
And early morning freezes,
Though a nip in the air,
May bring sniffles and sneezes.

But now the sweat trickles,
And drips from my nose.
And my sticky clothing tickles,
From my head to my toes.
Frost on the grass blades,
And fog form my breath,
Just thinking of these things,
Is causing me stress.

The summer sun blazes,
And gives no relief.
It burns and it crazes,
With misery and grief.
So bring on cool weather,

And college football!
Along about August,
I'm ready for fall.

Dexter C. Satterwhite Jr.

July 1992

Something to Think About

Looking for the truth;
Searching for my youth.
It seems I've lost them both.
Nothing comes to mind but an oath!

It makes me want swear,
When I think of where,
My life is going now,
And I think of how,
I'll put my child through school,
Unless I break the rules,
And how I'll ever save,
Enough to retire and not be depraved.

The world changes so fast.
Nothing seems to last.
No need to wonder why?
I'll just live until I die.
And when I'm dead and gone,
Someone else will come along,
To sit here in this place,
And occupy this very space,
And wonder why the world went by,
Until one day they up and die.

But, is it nothing more than folly,
To sit here in this melancholy,
Grasping for some abstract truth,
And pining for my long lost youth?
When the work of God's hand is everywhere,

And all His blessings I can share.
My problems pale before His might,
If I but face His guiding light,
And place my hand in His to hold,
And with it my mortal soul.

Though the setting sun brings a ting of sorrow,
It will rise again tomorrow.
And bring with it a clear new day,
So that I might make my way.

Dexter C. Satterwhite Jr.

October 1992

Middle Age Blues

"A day that will live in infamy,"
Like a nun that's facing a pregnancy,
Just take a look in the mirror.
All those wrinkles are getting clearer.

It seems you've lost a step,
And with it, most of your pep.
Yes, half your life is gone,
But only if you live that long.

It's all downhill from here.
Might as well sit down and have a beer.
There's nothing left but grief.
"Father Time" is a master thief.

He takes away the fire,
And with it your desire.
And all that's left to reap,
Is but a good night's sleep.

So when you're walking with a gimp,
And other things are getting limp,
And it's harder and harder to "party,"
Hey, "life begins at forty!"

Dexter C. Satterwhite Jr.

November 1992

Self-reflection

I've written poems to make you think,
And poems to make you laugh.
That this old boy was a poet,
Will be my epitaph.

⁓⧉⁓

Dexter C. Satterwhite Jr.

December 1992

The Breath of Charon

Of life and death, I know but one,
The other I know not.
'Tis fate that steers our worldly course,
And draws the curtain on life's plot.

Some fear death's lurking spectral head.
They wish to run away!
To forever push it far ahead,
And never reach that day.

Some see it as a release from pain.
Some see it as a curse.
Some see it as a beginning.
Some see it as an end or worse.

But I will meet it when it comes;
From it, I cannot flee.
Within the Word of God,
Lays my hope for Eternity.

By the Promise of our Savior,
By our Father and His Grace,
I fear not "The Breath of Charon,"
Cold upon my face.

Dexter C. Satterwhite Jr.

December 1992

To Amanda

Amanda, fair Amanda,
Thine eyes have seen the light.
Thy heart leads thee to lofty goals,
And dreams within thy sight.
And I am left to carry on,
The mundane and the trite.

But it is for thy good you go,
And that is how it must be.
No longer can I seek advice,
Or quip in revelry.
Nor have a sympathetic ear,
For my poor poetry.

Yes, I will miss thy shining face,
Thy sense of humor bright.
Thy common sense, unshaken faith,
In justice, truth, and right.
Thy trust in God our Father,
Christ our Savior and His Light.

I thank thee fair Amanda,
No finer Dame hath known.
So now you go to conquer worlds,

And I am left alone.
And I will miss thy company,
Right to the marrowbone.

Dexter C. Satterwhite Jr.

December 1992

What Do I Do When I'm Sexually Starved?

What do I do when I'm sexually starved?
Should I go out cruising in my car?
Or try my luck in a single's bar,
Hoping wit and charm will take me far?
But knowing things the way they are,
I'll just wish upon a star.

Dexter C. Satterwhite Jr.

December 1992

Honeymoon's End

My heart and soul, I give to you,
My time and wealth and patience too.
These twenty years that I've lived through,
I feel as though I have the flu.

***

Dexter C. Satterwhite Jr.

February 1993

True Love

Love, true love means many things,
Caring and sharing and diamond rings,
Bottles and diapers and static cling,
Tending cuts and bruises and fire ant stings.

Cleaning house and washing shirts,
Long cold evenings of helping with homework,
Watching them grow and start to flirt,
Watching them leave and feeling the hurt.

Living together till someone dies,
Looking to Heaven through tear-stained eyes,
Living on till in death, the other complies,
These are the places where true love lies.

Dexter C. Satterwhite Jr.

February 1993

Valentine Poem 1993

"To whom it may concern."
"Your wish is my command."
From this you can discern,
You're lucky I'm your man.

And that so long ago,
You made our God a vow.
And after all these years,
You've stayed with me somehow!

❧

Dexter C. Satterwhite Jr.

February 1993

Cross-Pollination

Behold the lovely grove of trees,
Whose pollen floats upon the breeze,
That makes me cough and hack and sneeze,
And gag and choke and gasp and wheeze.

The pollen slowly filters down,
To cover everything around,
Limb and leaf and twig and ground,
And assaults my nose without a sound.

No warning comes till it's too late,
Until I find there's no escape,
And I am in an awful state.
Nowhere to hide from "nasal rape!"

It violates my every breath,
This yellow, fragrant "kiss of death,"
'Till it's so bad I must confess,
It's a wonder I have a sinus left.

I cannot make the forest scene,
Without my antihistamine.
Plant fornication is quite obscene,
To one with the hay fever gene.

Dexter C. Satterwhite Jr.

May 1993

108

Marse Robert

Riding proudly on that great horse Traveller:
Truly a man of principal.
Fighting again and again against all odds,
Carrying the day or at least forcing a draw,
What a responsibility for those old shoulders,
With no help save your soldiers and yourself:
Those soldiers whom you truly loved,
And oh how they loved you,
But fortune did not bless them,
Nor yourself.

Almost always right save once:
Just shows that you were human and the task too great.

Not willing to profit from name and deeds,
As so many others did.
As I said, you were a man of principal,
True to that principal always.
And at life's end,
Going back to those desperate days,
Upon your dying lips, this question,
"Is A.P. Hill up yet?"

Dexter C. Satterwhite Jr.

August 1993

I Am Your Flag

I am your flag.
I have been the symbol of our nation for more than two hundred
years.
My brothers and sisters fly over our Nation's capital,
In state capitals,
At court houses,
At schools and churches,
And at our embassies in foreign lands.
Wherever Americans gather, we are there.

I am your flag.
My brothers and sisters have flown over our nation,
In times of peace and in times of war.
They flew at Yorktown when our nation was born.
They flew at Fort McHenry, New Orleans, and Veracruz.
They flew at Manassas, Chancellorsville, Gettysburg, and Appomattox,
When my countrymen fought each other.
They flew in Cuba and the Philippines.
They flew in France in the Argonne Forest,
And later at Omaha Beach, Bastogne,
And finally in Germany on the Elbe itself.
The tired hands of brave marines raised my brother on Mt. Suribachi,
And in Tokyo.
They flew in Korea, Vietnam, and the Kuwait desert.
Wherever Americans have fought and died for our country,
We have been there.

I am your flag.
But now I've grown old.
My colors have faded.

My edges are frayed.
Now my retirement is nigh.
I've done my part,
And I deserve to be retired with dignity.
Remember me and what I stand for.
Always honor my brothers and sisters,
For they honor you.

Dexter C. Satterwhite Jr.

September 1993

Bonehead

My head is made of bone.
It's solid through and through.
My memory, the coup has flown,
I don't know what to do!

I remember my wife.
I remember my child.
I remember my life,
And my life style.

I remember the year;
Nineteen Ninety-Four I think.
It could be the beer,
But I don't drink.

I'm getting older,
And maybe dumber.
My feet are getting colder.
Isn't life a bummer.

But I did remember,
Although lately it seems.
And if you were born in December,
It would fit this "rhyme scheme."

Dexter C. Satterwhite Jr.

April 1994

Business Sense

This is the story of an ambitious stripper,
Who had quite a way with a strap and a zipper!
And though she worked so very hard at her trade,
Success eluded her; no fame came her way.

So she thought and thought about what she could do.
Should she wiggle a new way or toss them a shoe?
Then it came in a flash of inspiration,
Just how to handle this perplexing situation.

Without one further thought or regret,
She pursued expansion of her "fixed assets."
She found a surgeon and then took on,
Ten pounds of plastic and silicon.

And now the rest of her career would commence,
With her new legitimate business expense.
And her shrewd accountant won her admiration,
By assigning them each the appropriate depreciation.

And her career has soared to new heights.
Now when she's on the stage, "Oh what a sight!"
Yet the IRS still found room to complain,
Claiming a clear case of "Capital Gain."

Dexter C. Satterwhite Jr.

April 1994

When I Was Small

Mother, when I was small and hurt myself,
You were always there to comfort me.
You never scolded.
You never criticized.
You just kissed me and made it better.

When I was lonely, you hugged me and were my friend.
When I was confused, you counseled me.
When I was sick, you sat up with me.
When I was hungry, you fed me.
When I was helpless and could do nothing but lay there and cry,
You cared for my every need.

And now, if you need me,
For anything, day or night,
I'll be there; this I swear.

Dexter C. Satterwhite Jr.

May 1994

Cool Dreams

I gaze across the valley,
To the roaring stream below.
I picture that stream frozen
And the valley cloaked in snow.

But now the summer wind's blowing,
Through the trees and on my face.
And the Middle Saint Vrain is flowing,
Through this beautiful place.

For you see, it's always summer,
When I make my presence known.
It is June or July when my schedule,
Will let me climb these steppingstones,

To the porch of Alta Monte,
Where from my cares my soul can flee.
And forever would I stay here,
If it could only be.

Dexter C. Satterwhite Jr.

June 1994

Dark Thoughts

The demons come at night,
When from gentle slumber,
I suddenly snap awake,
And realize my return to sleep,
Is as remote as my dream,
So abruptly interrupted.

The demons creep out of the night shadows,
At the edge of my room,
To sit leering at the foot of my bed.
Laughing with glee, they dance on my chest,
Crawl in one ear and out the other,
And fill my heart and soul with fear.

Every problem seems so magnified,
Every care so heavy.
Worries become terrors,
Until sweat forms on my brow,
And I feel like damp moss,
In a dry creek bed.

Nothing to do but wait it out;
The demons come at night.
And only the morning sun,

A hot shower,
And the clear thoughts of day,
Will drive them away.

Dexter C. Satterwhite Jr.

July 1994

Insurance Blues

My insurance agent is after me.
Policies are his game.
Yes, he smells blood; it's plain to see.
How did he get my name?

He's back there snapping at my heels.
There is no keeping him away.
I wish he knew just how it feels.
Just what I need: another premium to pay.

I have insurance on my life.
I have insurance on my health.
I have insurance against all strife,
And insurance for my wealth.

I have insurance on my house,
And insurance on my car.
I have insurance on my spouse.
There's never a policy very far,

Away when premiums are due.
I'm past insurance poor; I'm destitute!
If I had a good lawyer, I would sue,
And live my life quite resolute,

To take my chances as they come,
And press on with patience and endurance.
But that's not the way that it is done,
When it comes down to insurance.

So my insurance agent will have his way,
And I'll be wondering what to do?
I'm worth more dead than alive anyway.
Insurance agents have to make a living too!

Dexter C. Satterwhite Jr.

September 1994

That Holy Night

That Holy Night,
The Star shone bright,
And bathed the world,
In purest light.
And Christ was born,
Upon that morn,
To teach us what is right.

The Father knows,
Of mankind's woes,
And sent His Son,
To save our souls.
For we were lost,
In death's cold frost,
'Till He came to end the night.

And from above,
Like a "Descending Dove,"
He came to tell us,
Of God's "Sweet Love."
For by His Birth,
He came to earth,
To raise us in God's sight.

And our souls are won,
Because God's Son,
Waved our sins away,
And made us one,

In his love that morn,
When he was born,
To save us by God's might.

And now we know,
What our Savior knows,
And why we live,
With an inner glow.
For our Lord was born,
Upon that morn,
To bring us all "God's Light."

Dexter C. Satterwhite Jr.

October 1994

While You Were Out

While you were out the world went by,
One quarter of a turn.
And thousands starved in Africa,
As our western forests burned.

Now you're back in, and the world moves on,
And what is the significance?
It's plain to see I fear to say,
It won't make a bit of difference.

⁓⟡⁓

Dexter C. Satterwhite Jr.

September 1994

November Dying

November is dying.
As surely as death will take us all one day,
It slides into the pit of December,
Where winter waits.

And the leaves that remain are thin on the trees,
Like an old man's beard.
And the wind blows cold,
Under a pale sky,
Dotted with wispy clouds,
That swirl as they pass.
And the days grow short,
And brown and gray dominate the landscape,
Streaked by long shadows.

And my soul cries out for dying November:
And the dying sun,
And the dying world,
And the dying year,
And the cold wind,
And the deserted land,
And the long dead nights to come.

Dexter C. Satterwhite Jr.

November 1994

"Terence"

"Terence" wrote his poems of woe,
Of life's despair and death's release.
On and on the melancholy goes,
'Till I'm devoid of grief,
And longing for relief!

He never wrote a merry word,
Nor had a merry thought.
Of blooming bud or flying bird,
To him it mattered naught.
Self-pity's what he sought.

Never any good to come,
From anything beneath God's sky.
And nothing left to do but run,
Life's course until we die,
And decompose by-and-by.

But I know better; there is more.
Christ our Savior, 'tis through Him.
Though our souls be tossed on stormy shores,
Of misery and sin,
They will be gathered in.

So "Terence," I leave you to wallow,
In your sad and lonely state.

With all your verse I tried to swallow,
It did give me a "belly-ache."
You were right about that at any rate.

Dexter C. Satterwhite Jr.

January 1995

Anniversary Poem 1995

I almost forgot,
But not,
Quite this time.
So I wrote this rhyme,
To tell you of my love,
Though you may tell me to shove,
It where the "sun don't shine."

So now I surrender,
But I did remember,
With the help of your son,
The very one,
Who reminded me of the date,
Before it was too late,
Leaving me to my fate.

I do love you,
It's true.
So let's not wait,
And have a date,
On this special day,
What do you say?
Will you?

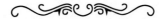

Dexter C. Satterwhite Jr.

July 1995

A Pleasant Interlude

Am I working hard? I'm fixing to.
It's something that I've got to do!
And I need to do it every day.
If I don't, there's hell to pay.

It gives me time to rest my eyes,
To sit and think and philosophy,
To solve the world's problems one by one,
To work them out until I'm done.

I think we tend to overlook,
The importance of this well used nook.
To take a rest and do our thing:
A chance to rejuvenate our brain.

But take some advice my fine young lad.
Too much of a good thing can be bad.
Too long a time upon the seat,
Removes the feeling in one's feet!

When you take your daily recreation,
Just remember this prudent observation.
It's fine to sit in contemplation:
But "all things in moderation."

Dexter C. Satterwhite Jr.

September 1995

Will?

Will autumn be autonomous,
After spring has finally sprung?
Will winter win us over,
Now that summer's come and gone?

Will the next year bring us promise,
As the green leaves show their face?
For now the cold wind blows them,
All over the flipping place.

Will the taxman come to plunder,
As he does year after year,
To rape the fruits of all my labor,
Leaving me in debt up to my ears?

Will I live to see the next year,
As down the road of life I go?
Or will the road just end abruptly?
Of this I do not wish to know.

Could I look into the future,
What unseen things would I see?
And what burdens would it bring me?
I thank God it's not meant to be.

Dexter C. Satterwhite Jr.

December 1995

Cycles

They were born, and they grew.
They learned and matured.
Their parents grew older,
But still they endured.

Then in time they left,
Because they were grown,
And went into the world,
To make a way of their own.

Then they met each other,
And their feelings emerged.
And before too long,
Their two lives converged.

And from this union,
New life can begin.
And the cycle repeats,
All over again.

Dexter C. Satterwhite Jr.

January 1996

So There

Well some of my poems are corny,
And some of my poems are trite.
But I'll tell you this by-golly-gee,
They sure were fun to write.

Dexter C. Satterwhite Jr.

March 1996

As You Walk to Emmaus

As you walk to Emmaus,
Please remember this one thing.
That each journey undertaken,
By foot, or car, or plane,
Requires the will to get there,
Which only comes from the heart,
And that Jesus, our Lord and Savior,
Is ready to do His part.

So journey on you brave traveler,
Seek His will along the way.
Seek His guidance as you wander,
And you'll never go astray.
Just remember that He loves you,
As only Christ our Lord can do.
And He'll be waiting there to greet you,
When the journey is through.

Dexter C. Satterwhite Jr.

July 1996

Dreams

Sometimes when we plan for the future,
We never seem to do what we plan.
We spend all our time in the planning,
Then our everyday life takes command.
So we put all our plans in the closet,
Along with our hopes it seems.
And we only let them out when we want to,
When we've the need for a wish and a dream.

So in time we grow old and we never,
Do the things that we've wanted to do.
We keep putting them off for tomorrow,
Until it's too late for me and for you.
Don't wait until then to get started.
Life's so short, much shorter than it seems.
Don't let "Father Time" catch you napping.
Memories are much better than dreams.

Dexter C. Satterwhite Jr.

November 1996

Aboriginal American Revenge

In fourteen hundred and ninety-three,
Columbus had to take a pee,
And cried to the whole world, "ooh-ooh-wee!"
"That burns!"
"Why did I name this place the Virgin Islands?"

Dexter C. Satterwhite

July 1998

Life is full of loss and pain,
As comes the sun and then the rain.
We pore out our love from our heart's core,
On those with two legs and those with four.

Yet time doth pass as tides are tossed,
As we survive so does our loss.
And down life's path of dust and stone,
We are left to tread alone.

But by God's Grace, He giveth hope,
And thus the means for us to cope.
It's always here; it cureth all.
It's on your wrist and on the wall.

Dexter C. Satterwhite Jr.

January 2004

Beginnings

These two souls through time and space,
Have come together in this place,
To give their word and take their vow,
To live a life together now.

To go as one past sun and moon,
Past winter's chill and sunny June,
Past springtime's birth and autumn's death,
Down through the years of time that's left,
Till they grow old and part their way,
Upon some distant day.

May God bless this union new,
But somehow old for in all truth,
Multitudes before through days of yore,
Have paved the way.

For these two souls will now impart,
The pathway to one beating heart.
And these two souls have now begun,
The journey of two souls to one.

Now I shall close and to them say,
Keep ever true and never stray.

God bless you both upon your way,
This day.

Dexter C. Satterwhite Jr.

February 2005

The Secret to Happiness

I learned the secret to happiness this morning,
While I was mulching a flowerbed.
I realized that in just two days,
It will be covered with mounds of fresh turned earth,
Where my cats have done their business.

You see, the secret to happiness and contentment,
Is making them happy and content.
It's as plain as the nose on my face,
And the claws on their feet.

Dexter C. Satterwhite Jr.

April 2005

Merging Waters

Life is like a river,
From source down to the sea,
As it winds its way along its course,
Past days of storm and lee.

In youth its rapids rush,
Over crag, and boulder and stone.
In time waters pool and eddy,
As they slowly meander along.

And tributaries merge,
Their waters as they flow,
Bringing their unique "cartage,"
To the down stream course below.

Just as rivers flow to the sea,
So do the lives of men,
Rushing through the rapids of youth,
To the estuary of life's end.

And just as tributaries merge,
To form a greater stream,
So do the lives of men and women,
Within the human theme.

Of what I speak is marriage,
The joining of two souls,
The union of man and woman,
In God's paternal fold.

For a man doth take a woman,
To be his wedded wife,
To share his triumphs and sorrows,
Down the twisting channel of life.

And they will be one with each other,
As through their lives they go.
Like the merging of two rivers,
Their combined waters flow.

Dexter C. Satterwhite Jr.

July 2006

Commitment

Take commitment to heart,
And your marriage will last.
Don't and it won't,
It's as simple as that.

Dexter C. Satterwhite Jr.

September 2006

Myself and Me

Of course its we,
Myself and me.
Because, you see,
We always agree.

Dexter C. Satterwhite Jr.

September 2006

The Family Tree

Consider, if you will, the family tree,
That grows in every village and town,
Spreading its branches all around,
Reaching forth from sea to sea.

It represents a family line,
The history of a pedigree,
A part of the human dichotomy,
That transcends both distance and time.

Yet in its beginning, it is only a seed,
That sprouts its shoot into the air,
And spreads its branches here and there,
High above mere bush or weed.

And as it grows through storm and lee,
It reaches up to meet the sun,
Making a place for everyone,
Recording each niche of the family.

We come this day to celebrate.
For this man and woman by their love,
And the grace of God above,
Have combined their two lives as one today.

And their new branch henceforth shall grow,
Spreading twig and leaf all around,
Above all dwelling on the ground,
Who plod through dust and mud and snow.

And thus a new life has begun,
In the Most High's Perfect Plan,
Set in place for His servant man,
Provided by His Perfect Son.

And so in human history,
This man and woman have claimed their place,
Established their position in destiny's race:
Their unique place in the family tree.

Dexter C. Satterwhite Jr.

May 2007

In Lieu of Flowers

Think of the worst job you can imagine,
Right out of your darkest nightmare.
Just one little thought brings out a cold sweat,
It might even cause a loss of hair.

Yet it's done for the most part by women,
Supposedly the weaker sex of the two.
Day after day, they toil away.
Why they do it, I haven't a clue.

She's the piston and ring of the division,
The timing belt of the Liberal Arts firm.
She's the sole of the shoe that plods us onward,
The wax that the candle burns.

Her work is not always exciting,
But necessary nevertheless.
Sometimes, she's taken for granted by others,
Myself included I must confess.

So its time I stand up for Nancy.
Without her I'd be in a mess.
At times like these when I stop and think,
I'd be lost with anyone less.

Dexter C. Satterwhite Jr.

September 2007

Prudent Advice

In years, you've lived two score and ten.
What goes around comes back again.
I cannot stop the hands of time,
With clever verse and pleasant rhyme.

Time presses onward; it will not delay.
Ever forward it takes us, day after day.
Never does it tarry; it never abides.
It moves ever onward like an incoming tide.

Your remaining life is yours to live,
Much love and kindness you've yet to give.
Make the most of it in every way.
Live to the fullest each hour and day.

Youth is a shadow; the present is nigh.
Old age will soon follow in years by-and-by.
Experience is our guide; my statement is true.
My years on this earth number three score save two.

Dexter C. Satterwhite Jr.

October 2007

Rebirth

Consider sodium and chlorine.
Separate, they're anything but safe.
Chlorine gas will melt your lungs,
Sodium in water will wreck the place.

But combined, they are quite harmless.
They literally undergo rebirth.
What is achieved from joining the two,
Is nothing less than "the salt of the earth."

The same is true with marriage.
A man and a woman wed.
Their lives are combined in this union,
And their former existence is shed.

So they change into something better,
As close as two peas in a pod.
Hand in hand they travel through life,
Till they're laid beneath the sod.

So we gather in celebration,
Of the union of these two souls.
May their happiness grow ever greater,
As the rest of their lives unfold.

Dexter C. Satterwhite Jr.

April 2009

Degrees

Consider, if you will, college degrees.
We toil and slave both night and day,
Casting all our free time away,
To obtain one of these.

It seemed to be in some distant age,
That graduation would roll around,
And presenting ourselves in cap and gown,
We'd stroll across the stage.

As though it is due to the season,
Those receiving the "Bachelor's Degree,"
Despite they're no different than you and me,
Transform into a "Person of Reason."

"Wisdom" is the gift of the "Master's Degree,"
That magically anoints the fevered brain,
If we are not completely insane,
After completing our various theses.

And finally "Understanding" is the prize,
Of the almighty "PhD,"
The most coveted of all the college degrees,
Which surely allows one's intellect to rise.

So here I stand under God's sky,
Having earned my precious degree,

Contemplating all that it means to me.
I'm a "Person of Wisdom,"
Though I can't "Understand" why?

Dexter C. Satterwhite Jr.

April 2010

Moving

What is moving? Let me see.
Something once at "Point A" is now at "Point B."
And as to distance, it matters not,
Whether across the nation or a parking lot.

Every item must be gotten,
Nothing overlooked and nothing forgotten.
Every map and every book,
Collected from each cranny and nook.

Boxes to be filled, folders to be found,
And everything else that's laying around:
Pencils and scissors, staples and erasers,
Markers and punches, highlighters and paper,

Desks and computers, printers and tables,
Diplomas and pictures, binders and labels,
Copiers and faxes, microwaves and scantrons,
Three cheers for moving; it's just so much fun!

So now in reflection, I need no more yearn,
For the move to be over and normality's return.
So thanks to all who lent a hand,
And brought us to the "Promised Land."

Dexter C. Satterwhite Jr.

October 2011

Seasons

Seasons come and seasons go,
As months pass by, and rivers flow.
And soon we come to realize,
The passing seasons of our lives:
Of springtime's birth and childhood themes,
Of youthful fun and teenage dreams.

In summertime, from home we leave,
To face responsibility.
We find someone for whom we care,
Some other life that we can share.
Then autumn comes upon the stage,
As we slip into middle age.
And winter's chill doth take its toll,
As we realize that we've grown old.

We ask our God that He may bless,
Our lives till we draw our last breath.
But in the end, what makes life rich,
Is having someone to share it with:
Someone to share life's joy and pain,
Someone's support through triumph and shame.

Now I shall close with this last thought,
Of human endeavor and happiness sought.

Seasons come and seasons go,
And time moves on, of this I know.

Dexter C. Satterwhite Jr.

May 2012

Caller I.D.

If it says unknown,
Then I'm unknown,
And I won't answer the phone.

Dexter C. Satterwhite Jr.

October 2012

A Poem Is Better Than a Card

A poem is better than a card,
For it doth come from the heart.
As the verses stop and start,
Our feelings thus are set apart.

Our busy modern Life,
Filled with confusion and strife,
Takes over our view the of world,
As our senses seem to unfurl.

So even though this message is late,
And somewhat slow in leaving the gate,
You are still the sister I love,
As witnessed by our Father Above.

So let me issue this message so true,
My thoughts at this moment are strictly on you.
May this next year bring you joy and bliss.
What more can you ask than this?

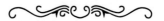

Dexter C. Satterwhite Jr.

April 2015

Driving Hard for Moscow

Driving hard for Moscow.
Trying to win the prize.
Pushing on with glorious visions,
Of victory in their eyes.

But winter fell,
A frigid hell,
To fight the battles in.
Through snow and rain,
What did they gain?
The long road to Berlin.

Dexter C. Satterwhite Jr.

January 2016

Consider

Consider this thing we call the heart.
Let us think it through that we may impart.
If love and kindness is its way,
Then misery and hatred will stay at bay.

Consider this thing we call the soul:
The part of our being within our control.
If we keep it pure as is God's will,
Then the work of our Father we can fulfill.

Consider this thing we call life,
Through joy, and sorrow, and hope, and strife.
It's a gift of the Lord, and we only have one,
To follow the footsteps of His Son.

Consider this being we call man:
The part of "Creation" we understand.
That man's not immortal, and death follows birth,
And thus understand our place on this earth.

Heart, soul, life, man:
I think you see,
There is a plan.

Dexter C. Satterwhite Jr.

March 2017

Phones

We finally got our new phones.
The latest that can be found.
So now we won't feel alone,
When eight o'clock rolls around.

They'll ring right off the hook,
With messages we must take.
And make us wish we took,
The day off at the lake.

The voicemail feature is great.
Now our students will bug us to death.
If only they could relate,
To the way we feel when we need rest.

Oh, our new phone system's just grand,
And we know we're going to love it.
Until we've had all we can stand,
And we tell Consolidated Communications to shove it!

Dexter C. Satterwhite Jr.

August 2017

Olivia

There are some people you can count on,
Time and time again.
Some people who will always stand by you,
Right to the bitter end.
Some people who are always there with you,
With a helping hand to lend.
There's a word we have for a person like this,
And it is simply friend.

Dexter C. Satterwhite Jr.

September 2017

Valentine Poem 2018

My wife, my love, the mother of my son,
My companion, my friend all rolled into one,
And now, I realize my life had begun,
When I chose you to be the right one.

Dexter C. Satterwhite Jr.

February 2018